M. C. Combs is a retired business executive who's been writing for various business publications for much of her career. She has published poetry and one military-based novel about her husband's profession as an aircraft accident investigator for the U.S. Navy and Marine Corps.

Darby, M. C. Combs' first work for young people was inspired by the life of a friend, a heroic military doctor who returned home with PTSD. She then saw the wonderful work that trained therapy horses are doing with our veterans with PTSD. The horses are changing lives, as are the people who create these therapy programs.

To U.S. Navy Commander John D. Harrah Jr. M.D.

M. C. Combs

DARBY, THE HORSE FROM HOPE

AUSTIN MACAULEY PUBLISHERS™

LONDON • CAMBRIDGE • NEW YORK • SHARJAH

Ordering Information:
Quantity sales: special discounts are available on quantity purchases by corporations, associations, and others. For details, contact the publisher at the address below.

Publisher's Cataloging-in-Publication data
Combs, M. C.
Darby, the Horse from Hope

ISBN 9781641826716 (Paperback)
ISBN 9781641826723 (Hardback)
ISBN 9781641826730 (E-Book)

The main category of the book: Biography & Autography / Educators

www.austinmacauley.com/us

First Published (2019)
Austin Macauley Publishers LLC
40 Wall Street, 28th Floor
New York, NY 10005
USA

mail-usa@austinmacauley.com
+1 (646) 5125767

Special thanks to Horses Helping People, HOPE, the Equine Therapy Program in Archer, Florida, and photographer Emily Rickert of Stereoscopic Productions, Dunnellon, Florida.

Chapter 1

It was a beautiful day in northern Florida. The sky was so blue and there was no sign of a cloud. The sunshine made the dark green grass in the pastures glisten as if little beams of light tipped every blade of grass. The big fields were surrounded by fences made of boards and painted dark brown. A big light-gray horse stood majestically in the pasture. His eyes were fixed on the huge, brown bird perched on a high limb of the tree just outside fence in the rear of the pasture. The bird's head was all white and the horse knew that this was not any ordinary bird. The bird was larger than any bird the horse had seen before.

For a moment, it was like the world was standing still. The bird's head was extended downward. The horse and the bird looked at each other. The bird knew that the big horse was no ordinary horse, and the horse sensed that he was seeing a very special bird. Their eyes met and they kept them locked on each other. The gray horse felt that the bird knew him and had a message he wanted to give him. He didn't know why the bird was there but knew it was an extraordinary moment and that things would never be quite the same.

After only a few minutes of the two animals staring at each other, the horse, whose name was Darby, felt a brief shiver as the huge bird blinked and lifted off the limb only to fly over the pasture. Then, he began to go higher and higher into the bright, blue sky. The bird's wings spread wide as he sailed into the air. Somehow, Darby knew he had just experienced something very special. *But what*, he wondered. *What was the bird trying to tell me?*

As the bird flew nearly out of sight, Julie, one of the people Darby knew, came running into the pasture. "Darby,

Darby," she called. "Did you see that bird? Did you see that enormous eagle? It looked like he was staring right at you."

The special moment over, Darby galloped over to Julie who was just opening the pasture gate. The horse raised and lowered his head in a firm 'yes' motion as he approached his friend. He was still thinking about the bird and feeling as if there had been a message he needed to understand, a message the bird had tried to deliver to him. Then, Darby thought that whatever it was the bird wanted him to know must be important. He decided right then that he would watch and wait until something happened to make it clear what the eagle had wanted to tell him. God's creatures communicate but the messages are not always clear, at first. *I will wait and watch,* Darby thought, *someday soon, I will know what he wanted me to understand.*

Julie attached a lead rope to Darby's halter and led him back to the big stable. The stable stood close to the road that people used to come and see Darby and the other horses. After all, Darby was no ordinary horse. Darby is a Therapy Horse.

This is also no ordinary place. This place is called HOPE. HOPE stands for HOrses helping PEople. Yes, Darby's job here is helping people, helping them find hope again. That's what a Therapy Horse does, explained the gentleman who was speaking to the group of children standing in front of Darby's stall.

As he was being introduced, Darby was thinking of how he wished he could explain it himself. Explain what he does for the people who come to HOPE for his help. *Since I can't talk, I have to depend on the people around me for introductions to my patients, but I can let you hear my thoughts as you are reading about HOPE and all that happens here.*

I can often show people how and what I am thinking by how I use my body. At that point, Darby had used his head and ears to illustrate what he was thinking. His ears stood up and faced forward and his head was positioned up and facing the people to create a strong and positive impression. He knew he was a handsome horse.

Terry, the Executive Director of HOPE, continued with the introductions. "Therapy horses are just like people who are therapists. The physical therapist helps people who have hurt their bones or muscles. A speech therapist helps people speak if they've forgotten how or had an injury that makes it harder. There are other types of therapists but I think you get the idea. A therapy horse helps people who have a number of difficulties. Sometimes, it is their brain that has been hurt or just didn't grow normally before they were born. Sometimes, it has been injured. Actually, horses can help lots of different people with different injuries or problems."

Terry paused, looked at Darby standing very erect and then he began walking and showing people the rest of the stable and the grounds. "People usually come to HOPE for our help. It is such a beautiful place. Sometimes, they just enjoy coming to our home and seeing the beautiful fields and trees and being in the outdoors. Some people just enjoy the serene views at our home here at HOPE."

In reality, thought Darby as the people with Terry had left the front of his stall, *mostly, people come to HOPE to see if we can help them. When they come the first time, most of them don't really believe that horses can help. That's usually because they've never been around horses and just see us as big animals that people can ride.*

Still, watching the people touring HOPE, Darby thought, *About now I bet those folks are wondering how horses can help people. First, most people don't understand that horses can think.* Darby laughed to himself, thinking of how some people act when they learn that horses are very smart. *They don't understand that all animals were created by God, we have all of the physical and mental skills we will need in life. Yes, I included mental skills. Horses are intelligent, not only able to think but to feel and react to those feelings.* Darby often got frustrated by the people who assumed that horses didn't understand what they said. Then, he shifted his attention to Julie, one of the HOPE volunteers who now had visitors with her.

"First, let me explain that the horses at HOPE are not just any horses," explained Julie. "They are all specially trained horses, trained to help people with many different issues," Julie continued talking and walking around with the people. Darby had heard this speech so often he could give it, if only he could talk. "Think of it as going to college to become a therapist," Julie said. "Each horse is selected by professional people who can tell they are very smart, kind, and care about people. Then they train the horses for each situation they may encounter."

What people don't understand, thought Darby, *while God didn't give horses the ability to talk, he did give us the ability to see, to listen, and to understand. We don't just understand the words but we know what people are feeling. That's usually better than understanding peoples' words. People aren't always truthful.*

Darby kept thinking about what he'd learned about people throughout his life. He'd learned even more during his training for this job. He laughed to himself as he remembered learning that most people usually don't want other people to know what they are feeling. *It has never occurred to people, if they've never known any of us, that horses know what they are feeling. We use our eyes, our ears and senses. That's our advantage, our senses.*

Most people don't have the ability to sense everything that is happening, before it can be seen. People depend most on seeing and hearing, ignoring what can be felt. I imagine God gave them this ability but most haven't fully developed it because they depend upon the 'big three', hearing, speaking, and smelling. *By the way*, he thought, *horses are good at smelling too*.

Most important is that therapy horses, in fact most horses, have a highly developed sense of awareness. Awareness requires using all of our senses at one time. Darby wondered why no one here ever told the people who come to HOPE about the horses' abilities to sense what and how people are feeling. *When working with a patient, I have to always be aware of what he or she is feeling,* Darby thought as he was pretending he was talking to the group that had just passed. *I'd be good at these introductions, if I could speak.* Darby found not being able to talk mildly inconvenient, but his thoughts were constantly coming and going.

Then he remembered that most riders of horses, when they first began to ride, may have heard someone say, "Remember you are in control. Let the horse know that you're the boss. A horse can sense if you are afraid of him." *Boy, is that right!* Darby mused. *Every horse I've met can sense how the person on his back is feeling about being there. Sometimes it's hard not to laugh with how people act when they first come here and then how different they are when they've learned enough to begin to ride.*

Oh, he thought, smiling inside, *people don't know that horses can laugh? Well, we can but we keep it inside. If you ever heard us laugh out loud, you'd be really afraid so we keep it inside. We love to laugh and frankly, people are sometimes really funny.* Just at that minute, Darby lifted his head and whinnied out loud. The people with Julie kind of jumped and then turned and looked at him. *Oh boy,* thought Darby. *That wasn't even a real laugh, just what people would call a giggle.*

Julie gave Darby a stern look as if to say, "Cut it out, Darby". *Oh, I'm being properly scolded with just that look,* Darby thought. *I bet she doesn't know that wasn't a real laugh. Oh, by the way, we keep our tears inside too. Sometimes, particularly in this job, people are very sad and while we cry with them, they don't know it. All we can really give them is to try and express our sympathy or empathy. That's usually what they need.*

Empathy, Darby thought, *that's when you can feel or at least understand what the person, or even another animal, is feeling. Empathy is really an important awareness when you're a therapy horse. Some people appear to be able to use their empathy. I have to know if a patient can feel empathy. That's another tool I use in my work.*

While the groom was bringing Darby his oats and hay for dinner, the big horse just kept thinking about how horses can let people know everything the therapy horse feels. Ignoring his dinner as he was still deep in thought, Darby was remembering his training. He was taught that if a patient is sad about something that has happened to someone else, like the loss of a family member, they need our sympathy. If something awful has happened to them personally, then they often need our empathy. Satisfied that he remembered his training well, Darby walked across his stall to his bucket of oats.

After his dinner and a long drink of water, Darby began to wonder about the new patient. Terry, the man who runs HOPE, had told him he'd be seeing them tomorrow. *Sounds like he's in pretty bad shape*, thought Darby. *A real challenge I guess. His name is Johnny*, Darby remembered. He has been a soldier and has served in two wars. He had seen and experienced so many very bad things in the wars that he has forgotten who he was.

Oh, Terry told me that he knows his name and where he had lived before he went to war, but he couldn't or didn't want to remember anything else or go back to his parents' house. All that was left in Johnny's mind were the bad things he had seen in the wars. Darby assumed, he had been wounded because he had been told that instead of going home after Johnny left the war, he was sent to a hospital to heal. The big horse assumed they were physical wounds, but he'd soon learn that they were not.

Darby found out later that once the hospital had done all they could for Johnny, he didn't want to remember a home. There could have been many reasons for that but now Johnny was homeless.

The big horse knew that there was a group of former soldiers that came to HOPE every week. A man named Bryan would bring them and that was who was bringing Johnny. Some of his fellow soldiers had taken Johnny to a home for soldiers who had no place else to go. The home was called Honor House.

Everyone at HOPE, including the horses, knew that everyone who lived at Honor House had been soldiers. Darby thought that like the other soldiers he'd worked with, Johnny felt better at Honor House. He must know that at least some of the people there understood who he had become. *He must still feel very lonely there*, thought Darby. You see, Johnny had no family of his own, no wife or children. That was a rule at Honor House. Darby soon learned that while his parents had tried, they couldn't seem to find their son in him.

Chapter 2

The next day, Darby was standing in his stall watching the rain coming down outside the stable. It had been a gray day and now a steady rain was falling. He'd been hanging out in the pasture but once the clouds gathered one of the lady volunteers, who come to help out at HOPE, came to get Darby and take him to the stable. Darby listened as she explained that he had a patient coming and she didn't want him to be all wet but look his best when they met. She'd even brushed him to make sure he'd be his handsome self. Darby knew what she was thinking.

Just after the rain stopped, a car drove into the parking area. Three men got out and walked toward the stable. Two of the ladies who volunteered at HOPE walked over and spoke with them. Darby could see this because they were standing in the aisle of the stable to keep out of the damp grass. He had seen the white-haired man before. That was Bryan and when he came to HOPE he always brought other men with him. Some of them came back many times, while some never returned after one visit.

Julie, the volunteer, took one of the men by the arm and led him over to Darby's stall. The big horse stepped over and reached his head out hoping she'd introduce him to the man. You see, in the stable each horse's stall's door has two parts. When the bottom half of the door is closed keeping the horse in the stall, the top half of the door can remain open, so the horses can see what is going on in the stable. They can actually reach their heads out to see the other horses and visit with the people in the aisle of the stable.

Julie walked a man over to Darby's stall. He was about six feet tall, slender, and with dark hair and eyes. His face was blank, and his eyes just stared ahead like he didn't even see Darby. It didn't take Darby long to understand why the man was here. Julie introduced the man to Darby. His name was Johnny and he was to be Darby's patient. She didn't say the patient part, but Darby knew. As Johnny stood there not wanting to make any contact with anyone, Darby took his nose and nuzzled Johnny's shoulder. He jumped at first but then looked right at Darby as he backed up. It hadn't frightened him, it had disturbed him and forced him to acknowledge the horse and mentally join Julie and Darby. Before, it had seemed he was in his own world, with no awareness of where he was and what he was about to do. Now he had joined them in his mind.

Julie pretended nothing had happened and continued the introduction. "Johnny, this is Darby. I can tell he wants to get to know you. That's why he nuzzled you. Would you speak to him, so he knows you are acknowledging him?" Julie continued like this was a normal introduction.

In fact, there is no such thing as a normal introduction. Everyone who comes to HOPE reacts differently when introduced to their therapy horse.

Darby thought, *I need to get more than a glance from Johnny. I need him to speak to me. So, I will nuzzle him again, this time on the side of his neck. Just try and ignore this.* Johnny jumped a little and started to swat my nose away only to stop before his hand reached me. He raised his eyes and looked at me for the first time and as his hand came up, instead of a swat I felt it slide down the front of my nose. *Round one,* Darby thought, *and I won.*

Darby's eyes fixed on Johnny's eyes as he heard Julie say, "He likes you. I can tell." *She always says that when there is a connection made between the horse and the patient,* thought Darby. Those words almost always continue to break the ice. You see, everyone likes to know that someone or some animal likes them. That's always true, people and horses and all of God's creatures.

Darby watched and saw that Johnny's eyes had gone blank again. Darby noticed that when Johnny realized that the big horse was looking directly into his eyes, he turned his head and looked away. *Okay,* Darby thought, *it's time to get to work. This man really needs me.*

"Pet his nose and forehead," Julie said as she lifted Johnny's hand up to Darby's face. "He loves to have someone rub his face, his jaw, and then to pet him on his neck." She continued to guide Johnny's hand as she could tell he wasn't going to follow her instructions himself. As Johnny's hand reached Darby's neck, he stretched out his head and nuzzled Johnny's neck again. At first he jumped a little but Darby didn't move and in a second or two he relaxed as Darby's head laid on his shoulder and leaned into the left side of his face. *Step one complete*, Darby thought.

As Johnny continued to pet Darby's neck, Julie had gone to get a lead to connect to Darby's halter. "Here Johnny," Julie said, as she handed him the lead. "Connect this to the ring on his halter under his chin and we'll bring him out of his stall and I'll teach you to brush him."

Here we go, thought Darby, *only a few minutes and we're on to step two*. Darby looked at Johnny's eyes again. Still blank. *Well, I've got to make some serious progress with him or he'll be a one-time visitor*, Darby thought.

Julie showed Johnny how to lead Darby out of his stall and into the aisle. "You hold his lead with one hand about eight inches from the halter and with your other hand, hold the lead off the ground, about a yard and a half from your first hand." Johnny took the lead and Julie told him, "That's right. You act like you've done this before."

Still, no reaction from Johnny as he led Darby out of his stall and into the aisle. Julie showed him how to find the two ropes attached to the two sides of the aisle and attach them to Darby's halter. Then he unhooked the original lead. Darby stood perfectly still as Julie went to get the brush and began to show Johnny how to brush Darby's neck. During this process Darby was beginning to think how he could overcome what seemed to be Johnny's lack of interest in this process.

After Julie showed Johnny how to move on to Darby's side, she stepped away to watch him brush, first one side of

Darby's back then his other side. *Okay, here we go,* thought Darby as he threw his head around to get Johnny's attention. Johnny stopped brushing and reached up and scratched Darby's nose. Darby then expressed his pleasure with a loud whinny, so loud that Johnny jumped a bit again.

"That's just Darby's way of saying thanks for the scratch," said Julie. "He really likes you. Darby isn't usually so vocal."

Thanks Julie, thought Darby, as he moved his head back to look forward only to be surprised. Johnny had stepped around in front of him. He was still petting Darby's nose. Darby looked into his eyes again and there was ever so slightly a change. Johnny was actually looking at Darby; looking at him in the eyes.

"Talk to him," said Julie, as she too was seeing some melting of Johnny's expression. "Talk to him," she continued. "Darby is the best listener I know." At that, Darby moved his head up and down as if to say, "Yeah, I'm a great listener and I can be a great friend".

"See what I mean, he's telling you he agrees with me, about being a great listener," Julie said as she moved to Darby's other side, motioning to Johnny that he had Darby's other side to finish brushing. And brush Darby he did.

"Would you like to lead him out to the pasture? It has stopped raining, and I'm sure Darby would enjoy a chance to run and graze a little now that the rain has cooled the air," Julie asked as she reached for the lead. She didn't bother to wait for an answer as she handed Johnny the lead and watched him unhook Darby from the aisle ropes.

Johnny seemed focused on holding the lead just as Julie had shown him, before and the three of them walked slowly out of the barn towards the far pasture. Darby was glad Julie had selected that pasture as it gave him more time with his patient. HOPE had four large and well fenced pastures, three big paddocks and a riding ring. It took several minutes to walk to the pasture and Julie began to slow down and then stop, to watch as the horse and patient walked on. Johnny was paying a great deal of attention to the position of his hands on the lead but slowly, his grip began to loosen as he became more comfortable and relaxed.

Darby walked slowly to have more time with Johnny and when they reached the gate he turned and nuzzled Johnny again as if to say "Thanks". They stood in front of the gate for a couple of minutes and Darby focused his eyes on Johnny, giving him a long look. Then putting his head over Johnny's shoulder and stood there as if to say, "Come back and see me. I really like you and we can be friends". Johnny just stood there, not moving, not pulling away from Darby but just feeling the big horse's head resting on his shoulder.

"Thanks Darby," Johnny said quietly and then he stepped over and opened the gate.

Darby was thrilled as he and Johnny walked into the pasture. Johnny unhooked the lead and stepped out, closing the gate. Darby just stood there as if to say, "You don't have to leave me now. If you want to talk, I'm here for you." Johnny stood there, not saying a word for several minutes before speaking.

"I'll be back to see you Darby," Johnny said as he looked Darby right in the eye. "Next time, I'll bring an apple or a carrot for you. Which do you like better? Would you like a carrot? Or an apple." As the word apple came out of Johnny's mouth, Darby whinnied and shook his head up and down. "You do listen, so an apple it will be," Johnny quietly said reaching out his hand to Darby and patting his nose again.

Darby kicked up his heels and galloped off, then turning to see Johnny walking back to meet Julie. *We did it*, Darby thought. *He'll be back, and this is one patient I think we can help*. Nothing makes a therapy horse happier than knowing he's made a friend of a patient.

Darby came back to the fence and saw that Julie had walked Johnny over to the riding ring. The other man who had come from the Honor House had been coming to HOPE for a number of weeks. He was on Betsy, the big bay mare. Darby thought he remembered that the man's name was Bill.

Bill was riding Betsy around the ring with no saddle, only two saddle blankets. He had learned to trust Betsy so much that he was lying backwards with his head on her rump. Johnny stood outside the ring and watched. Bill had tried to tell him in the car on the way to HOPE how much he liked Betsy and how good she made him feel about himself. Johnny hadn't believed it but here was a real demonstration of what Bill had meant.

"I could never do that," Johnny said out loud, even though he'd meant to keep that thought to himself.

"We'll see," said Julie so quietly that Johnny barely heard her.

Darby had been watching Johnny by the ring and thinking, *that's nothing Johnny, we'll go there and much farther. You'll come back to who you used to be or maybe even better. Who do you want to be in your future?* Darby knew that, as he was now, Johnny didn't have much of a future. He had to find himself again and decide who he wanted to be. Darby had seen lots of guys like Johnny and had actually been able to help some. Some were just too far into another world to find their way back and even Darby hadn't been able to bring them back.

Darby didn't know much about war, only what his patients had told him. That was enough for this horse to know that it caused some people to lose their lives, while others seemed to lose their souls. Strangely, those who lived often wished that they too had died. *I guess living without a soul is worse than not living at all*, thought Darby. But if that soul is down there, even a little of it left, we'll find it, my patient and I. *We'll find it Johnny*, Darby thought as he sauntered over to the watering barrel where he took a long drink. *Now for my exercise*, Darby thought as he began running across the pasture.

Chapter 3

Darby usually had two patients a day. One in the morning and another in the afternoon. The amount of time he spends with them depends on just how far he has progressed in their therapy. For some reason that he couldn't explain, Darby found himself thinking about Johnny in his spare time and planning their next visit. There's something about this guy that feels different, his need for help seems even greater than most. *How do I get him to open up? Somehow, I feel like I don't have much time. There's something desperate about him.* Darby could sense it and no one else seems to know.

The veterans from Honor House usually came to HOPE on Wednesday afternoons. By Wednesday Darby had his plan for Johnny's visit well defined. *I don't think he can wait and go through the therapy over many weeks*, Darby thought. *The staff here won't understand but I have to move more quickly with Johnny. He needs me more than most who come to HOPE.* As he stood in his stall on Tuesday evening waiting for his dinner, Darby hatched a plan.

The next morning, Terry, the Executive Director of HOPE, walked past Darby's stall. Darby reached out his long neck and nipped at Terry's shirt sleeve. Terry turned quickly with a look of surprise on his face. Then, his expression softened as he looked at Darby.

"What do you want boy?" Terry said as he turned toward the big gray horse. He's learned to trust Darby as he had once been his patient and he knew that Darby would communicate any way he could. In fact, he often credited his recovery to Darby's patience and unique ability to create trust with his patients. Terry had been in the War in Iraq and came to HOPE for help living with PTSD or possibly getting over it, as much as someone can.

"Darby, is there something on your mind?" Terry asked. At that question, Darby began nodding his head up and down. He knew that was the answer "Yes". Then, Darby showed Terry that he needed to get out of his stall in order to answer Terry's question. He took his teeth and tried to slide the bar that kept his stall door closed.

"You want out boy? Where do you want to go?" Terry asked as he moved to open Darby's stall door. Darby walked out of his stall and out of the barn with Terry following close behind. Darby stopped in front of the HOPE office door and tried to open the door knob with his teeth.

"Is there something in the office you want?" Terry wondered out loud. Darby immediately said, "Yes" with an up and down head shake. "Fellow, no therapy horse has ever asked to go into the office," Terry whispered into Darby's ears that now faced forward. "Okay boy, you stay outside, and I'll get what you want. Now, we've got to figure out what you need. Is it about one of your patients?" Again the up and down head movement by Darby.

"Which one Darby?" asked Terry. "I've got it. I'll read the list of your patients and you can tell me when I've read the right name. Okay?" Again, a yes from Darby. Terry went into the office and into his desk. He pulled out a piece of paper, went back to the front door and started reading the names of Darby's patients. The big horse kept his head very still until Terry read Johnny's name, John Harris. Darby nodded aggressively so that Terry couldn't miss that this was the patient he was concerned about.

"What do you want with this?" Terry asked more to himself than Darby. "Oh, I've got it, today is Wednesday and Johnny should be here. You want me to read you his background that the Honor House put on his application for therapy here at HOPE." Once again, Terry returned to his desk, this time into the largest drawer. After searching for a moment, he pulled out a folder, opened it and returned to where Darby was standing. Terry began reading. Darby listened intently to every word.

"Name is Major John Harris, MD. He's a doctor Darby," said Terry looking up at the big gray horse. "He's a doctor! His service record says he served in forward aid stations in Iraq with the Air Force for two tours. A tour can be from six months to a year at a time, Darby." Terry wanted Darby to understand each word. Then he read on.

"After four years in the Air Force, serving as a doctor, he left the service. Next, he went back to being a hospital Emergency Room Doctor. That was his specialty and it also explains why he served in the forward aid stations in the war zones in Iraq. Then he went back for another specialty and he studied Hyperbaric Medicine. That's strange Darby. That's a specialty that involves using water and ambient pressure for healing and also how humans deal with being in deep water or in water for a long period of time." Terry read on, not particularly to Darby but because what he found was so interesting.

"Okay, now I understand Darby," Terry said as he looked up at the big horse standing in the office door. Terry didn't think about it being strange that Darby was now almost in his office but was more focused on what he'd found in Johnny's history. "Darby, then Johnny joined the Navy. He went on to serve for several years with Seal Teams. Darby, Seals are the toughest of the tough and do the most dangerous missions of any one in the military and there was Johnny taking care of them. Darby, I can't even imagine what Johnny must have seen and been through in either Iraq or while he was with the Seal Teams."

WOW, thought Darby as he stepped over to Terry and nuzzled his neck. "Thanks Darby," said Terry. "If you hadn't brought me here we'd have never known how much Johnny needs our care. That's your care Darby and now that you know and understand how damaged Johnny likely is, it's up to you to help him."

Then Terry realized that the big horse was standing in his office. He'd been so interested in Johnny's history that he hadn't noticed that Darby had wanted to get closer so he could hear everything Terry read off the paper. Now he knew. Not all of it but Darby understood that Johnny was probably very disturbed by all he had been through. Darby thought that Johnny might be one of those men who had lost their soul and no longer allowed themselves to feel anything.

Darby backed out of the office as there wasn't room there for him to turn around. Terry followed him, marveling at the clear demands Darby had made to learn more about his patient. *Now*, Terry thought, *it will be fascinating to see how Darby uses that information to help his patient.*

Darby only had a few hours now to develop a therapy plan for Johnny. It couldn't be therapy as usual. Darby knew there was an urgency to make a break-through with Johnny. The more he had thought about their first time together, the more he was aware that Johnny was in serious trouble. He had been injured badly. It was not an injury you could see but it was very serious, nevertheless.

Darby was almost grateful that his morning patient had not been able to come to HOPE that day. They said she had the flu but it gave Darby the next three hours to plan his time with Johnny. Julie stopped by his stall after she'd had a meeting with Terry.

"Darby, what you did this morning was amazing" Julie said. "Terry told me to let you take the lead today when Johnny comes. He also told me about Johnny's background. You've got your work cut out for you Darby," she said as she walked away toward the office where Terry had called a meeting of the staff and volunteers.

Chapter 4

While he waited for Johnny to come for his therapy session, Darby began to think about why he cared so much. He let his mind wander to when he was very young. Then, he remembered that he would have let all of this power to be in control over a person's recovery go to his head.

Darby began thinking through his own life story. *I was born on a thoroughbred farm called Field of Dreams in Ocala, Florida. This was a very successful farm at breeding and raising race horses. My father was a champion race horse and my mother had given birth to several very successful brothers. By successful, I mean they were winners in big time races. Every spring, the farm would have over a dozen foals, that's what baby horses are called.*

By the time we were a year-old, the colts, that's the young male horses, and the fillies, the young female horses, would be put into a special pasture where we could run and play. During that year each yearling would be taken to the track and we would begin our training to be a race horse.

I learned a lot but I didn't show much talent on the race track. In fact, I didn't really like running around in big circles while the people timed me and would meet and shake their heads. I didn't like someone on my back using their crop, that's a leather like stick, hitting me on the rump to make me go faster. After several months of working with me, it was clear to the owners and trainer that I was not going to be a champion race horse. I remember being a little depressed about it but I was glad when I didn't get taken from the pasture to the track every day.

I liked playing and running in the pasture, just having a good time and no responsibilities. Once and a while, as the other yearlings were leaving the pasture to go to the track, I was a little sad that I had been such a disappointment to my trainer. I had really tried to run as fast as I could, Darby thought *but it was never good enough.*

By the time I was a two-year-old, I was for sale. Potential buyers would come and go or select one of the other two-year-olds. My depression grew deeper, and I stopped caring about anything. It had never occurred to me that no one would want me. Just like it often happens with young people, I became stubborn and began to behave badly.

I remember one day when I was taken to a pasture while all of the other colts and fillies my age were moved to another pasture. I was alone, and I hated it. There I was, in a field and I was kept there by fences made of boards. Suddenly, I wondered why I'd never wanted out of that pasture before. I began to think about how I could get out and go be with the others. Suddenly, I began to run toward the fence, launched myself with my hind legs and sailed over the fence. Boy, I remember how good that felt, flying in the air, if for only a moment.

One of the grooms, the people who take care of the horses, saw me jump the fence and go running off towards my friends. The farm's owner was just walking up to discuss something with the groom.

I remember the groom taking his hat off and hitting his leg with it.

He said, "Sir, did you see that? Did you see Darby jump that five-foot fence? He sailed over it. Had to be a six-foot jump."

Both men then ran to catch me to put me back in the pasture, Darby remembered. *Once in the pasture, when I thought no one was looking, I remember jumping the fence again. I didn't know it, but the owner had been looking from the corner of the two-year-old's barn.*

"Well, I guess we've found what Darby is good at," he said to no one in particular. "Boy, that horse can jump!"

With that my career was determined.

Still deep in thoughts of his past, Darby remembered that it was only a few days after he took those jumps that a lady with a saddle over her arm came into the barn. She was with the owner and they came directly to his stall. "He's quite a jumper, this one. He's just turned two and cleared the pasture fence by a foot. Of course, he's never done it with a rider but the grooms say he's the smartest horse in the two year's barn. Why don't you take him out for a ride?"

That day Darby got used to a different type of saddle and quickly learned how to impress a rider. "I like how he moves," the lady said to the owner. "He'll need a lot of training but if he can jump like you say, he might be ideal for a successful hunter. I like his size; did you say he was 17 hands? (If you need to know, a hand equals four inches so if you multiply four by 17 that's how tall he is. The measurement is taken from the ground to the horse's withers, what you might call his shoulders.)

"Let's put him in the pasture and see if he's in a mood to jump today. He was pretty impressive, the other day, when he flew over those fences like he had wings." The owner was in his selling mode. Darby had seen that before and he kind of liked the lady and jumping was just plain fun.

Darby decided it was time to show off. Once in the pasture he started a powerful gallop and as he reached the fence he propelled himself as high as he could and landed perfectly on the other side. Then, he galloped on and jumped into the next pasture where the yearlings were. Once there, he wondered if he had been good enough. So, he stopped short and looked back to see what the people thought. Darby was smiling inside remembering that day.

"Wow!" said the lady. "He's also smart and a real show off." She turned to the owner and asked, "How much do you want for him?" Darby's fate was sealed. He was going to be a jumping horse.

Chapter 5

As Darby stood waiting for Johnny to arrive, he kept his mind back in his past. *For the first time, I knew how it felt to be really good at something. I could jump! I wonder if Johnny has ever felt good about what he did. Gosh, he was a Doctor, you'd have to feel good about helping people. I sure do. I've got to get him to tell me. Maybe he can recapture some of that feeling.*

Oh, there comes the car from the Honor House. What if Johnny didn't come back, worried Darby. The car stopped and both Bill and Johnny got out of the back seat. Bryan, the manager of the Honor House had brought another new patient with him today.

Darby had been so deep in thought that he hadn't noticed that Julie was back today too. *Great,* he thought, *now to work.* Julie took Johnny aside, welcomed him back and guided him into the tack room. *Okay,* thought Darby, *now he gets the people guidance. She'll tell him how we can really be the most successful in his therapy and how we can work with me to gain the most confidence in his therapy.*

After about ten minutes, Johnny came out of the Tack Room with a lead in his hand and headed right for Darby. The big gray horse gave Johnny a big nod and whinny, to say hello and welcome back. His eyes were blank again. *Oh no*, thought Darby, *it looks like we have to start all over.*

As Johnny began to open the stall door Darby reached out his neck and nuzzled Johnny's neck. *No reaction*, thought Darby. *Okay, let's play it straight for a few minutes and see if Johnny will look at me.* Johnny got the brush and brushed Darby all over but never once let his eyes meet Darby's. Just as Johnny was reattaching the lead, Darby spotted a bulge in

Johnny left pants pocket. *Okay fellow,* thought Darby, *you can't fool me, that's my apple and I think I'm going to use that to get your attention. I'm tired of him acting like a zombie today.*

Just then Darby moved his head down and bumped the bulge in the pocket with him nose. Johnny jumped. "What are you doing?" Johnny said in a startled voice. "What's wrong with you today?"

That got his attention, Darby thought, *but I'm not sure it was the kind of attention I wanted.* Just then Darby saw Johnny's put his hand in the pocket that Darby had bumped.

"Oh, I get it," said Johnny as an actual smile came over his face. "Darby, you knew what was in my pocket, you rascal. You want the apple." As Johnny patted the outside of his pocket he looked right in Darby's eyes and said, "That, my friend, is for later. As for now we are supposed to take a walk around the farm. "

Hallelujah, thought Darby. *He's alive and now we can get to work.* Darby stepped aside and began to walk properly beside Johnny. Darby thought, *Okay fellow now I've got to get you to trust me enough to start to talk.* Then Darby started to walk faster and faster.

"Hey fellow," said Johnny as he was almost running to keep up. "What's your hurry? Slow down, will you?"

Darby immediately slowed to the walking pace they had before. "That's a good guy," said Johnny who was almost panting from running beside Darby.

Now he knows I listen and will do what he asks, Darby thought. Now, while that wasn't enough to be sure of his trust, it's a step in the right direction. Darby slowed down to a complete stop which startled Johnny, who turned and looked at Darby in the eyes.

"What's wrong boy," asked Johnny. "Why did you stop?" At that question Darby tilted his head, still looking Johnny in the eyes. He made sure his ears were facing forward. Then Darby carefully placed his right front hoof a little forward of his other hoof. Then he lifted it slightly, as if it was hurt.

Johnny watched carefully. "Is it your foot Darby? Did you hurt your foot? Let's take a few steps and let me see how you're walking." Johnny moved his hand up on the lead and gently tugged. Darby took two steps making sure to put little weight on his right front foot. *It was a great imitation of being lame*, Darby thought.

Johnny bent down and felt Darby's leg. "I don't feel any problem," Johnny said as if he was talking to a patient. "Let me see your hoof. Maybe you got a stone in your hoof." Johnny carefully lifted Darby's hoof and looked at it feeling around Darby's shoe. "Look's okay, boy but you may have gotten a bruise when we were walking." Johnny carefully replaced Darby's foot on the ground and Darby cooperated with the entire examination.

That's what he needed, thought Darby. *He needs to think of me as his patient. He reacted like a doctor and now I have to keep playing lame. That's okay, I can fake a limp for a while.* Just then he saw Julie coming out to meet them.

"What happened," asked Julie? "Is Darby alright?"

"He seems to have become a little lame," Johnny told her. "I can't find anything wrong but he may have stepped on a stone. It isn't there now but he's acting like he might have a bruised foot. I'll walk him back."

"Take him to the wash rack on the other side of the barn. Let's cool him off a bit," said Julie. "I'll go get you a sponge and scraper and will show you how to bath him," she called back as she ran on to the barn.

Darby stood there trying to look pained and Johnny stepped over to him and ran his hand down Darby's neck. The horse moved his head over to Johnny' shoulder and rested his head against Johnny's neck like he was trying to say "Thanks". They stood there for a couple of minutes, Johnny continuing to pet Darby's neck. *Boy, this is quite a moment* Darby thought. *That's what it took. He needed to be needed. Now to limp all the way back.*

"Darby, I used to be a doctor," Johnny said quietly as they walked. "I'm not anymore and never will be again, but I guess my past just took over." Darby stopped and stepped around

31

Johnny to look him in the eyes again. "I know, I know, no one believes I can just quit being a doctor, but I have. I hate being put in the position of trying to save lives because sometimes..." Johnny lowered his head and his eyes. "Sometimes Darby, you just can't. Darby, you can't imagine how terrible it feels when you can't save someone."

He paused a few minutes and from his eyes it looked like he was a million miles away. Then after a few minutes Johnny said, "I don't ever want to be in that position again, trying to play God and failing. Just can't ever do that again. I hate who I am, I hate it." Johnny's voice cracked, and Darby saw tears welling up in his eyes.

Whoa, thought Darby, *he's in real pain.* Darby put his head on Johnny's shoulder as if to say, "I understand and I'm here for you." Johnny reached up and put his hand up to Darby's mane and seemed to hold on.

"Thanks boy," said Johnny. "You're a good friend and somehow I think you understand. I guess we need to get back to the wash rack." They began to walk back to the barn and Darby saw Johnny take his hand from the short portion of the lead and wipe his eyes.

Oops, thought Darby, *I almost forgot to limp. I hope nobody noticed but that little bit of faking was worth it to make that kind of break-through so early in our relationship.* They walked on, Darby limping ever so slightly. After the bath, which Darby really enjoyed, Johnny seemed to lighten up as well. Julie came around the barn and told Johnny that Bryan and Bill were getting ready to leave and go back to Honor House.

"Let me take Darby back to his stall," Johnny called to Julie and the other men who were waiting on Johnny to leave. Just before Johnny put Darby in his stall, the big horse nudged Johnny's pocket, the one that held the something round. "Oh, I almost forgot that I brought you something," said Johnny. "Thanks for reminding me Darby." Then, Johnny pulled a big red apple from his pocket. "Is this what you want big guy?" Johnny said as he held the apple up in front of Darby.

Darby shook his head up and down in a definite declaration of 'yes'. Johnny reached over and hugged Darby around his neck and then put the apple up to his mouth. "See you next week buddy. You take care of that foot because we have more work to do on my next visit. Julie has said that next week I am ready to start to learn to ride." Johnny called back as he walked to the Honor House car.

Feeling very satisfied with himself, Darby crunched and swallowed the apple in no time. And went to his water pail for a drink. Julie and the Director, Terry, were opening his stall door when he turned back around. "Let me look at that foot," Terry said as he reached down to Darby's leg. He felt Darby's leg and lifted his foot. When Darby put his foot back down it was clear to Terry that it was not tender. "Okay Darby, were you playing lame for a reason?"

Darby gave a quick nod which Terry understood. "Had a good day with Johnny, huh?" There was another quick nod from Darby and Terry left the stall smiling. He turned around to Darby and said, "You rascal you." Darby knew that Terry understood that Johnny had been a doctor. "He maybe needed a patient, right? Good boy Darby."

As Terry walked away, Darby was feeling very proud of himself, not for what Terry had said but because he'd had a small success. Johnny had already started to open up. Darby really liked this man and felt bad for him as he seemed so lonely. Darby wondered if he could talk to anyone at Honor House or if he just kept to himself, alone.

Johnny continued to come to HOPE every week. He'd learned to care for Darby and to ride in the ring. He trusted Darby not only to ride but as someone with whom he could share all his pain and terrible memories. Johnny had found that when he spoke about them out loud to Darby, they didn't keep coming back into his mind, over and over. It was like talking to Darby about something, that haunted him, was like setting it free, getting it out of his brain. His bad dreams didn't wake him every night. Oh, there would still be bad dreams, just not so often.

Weeks later Johnny told Darby that before coming to Honor House, the group of men, who were depressed like he was, had gone on a very long hike. They'd walked from the southern to the northern borders of the United States. "They were all like me and had lost all hope of ever living a normal life again," Johnny had explained. "It helped while we were hiking but as soon as the walk was over, all the nightmares and struggles came back."

The day the hike ended, and it had taken three months, one of the other guys had asked Johnny to join a group of them who were going to live at the Honor House in Florida. They said it might be good for Johnny to go to a place called HOPE. All he knew about it was that there were horses there.

Darby remembered that when he and Johnny had first met, he didn't know any of this about Johnny but as they spent time together, he had shared it all with his therapy horse. Darby wondered if people really knew what great listeners horses can be. The big gray horse thought back to his training. He'd been told, "Sometimes, the therapy patients don't feel comfortable talking to other people but because they know you can't tell their secrets, they feel comfortable sharing them with you, their therapist."

Chapter 6

Darby had learned to enjoy any small success and understood that being successful on one day was not necessarily a guarantee of continued success. Each day was another opportunity to try to do things well and make his patients feel better. That evening after his dinner, Darby began to think back about his earlier successes and his failures. *When you're older and look back on your life, things look different*, he thought.

His mind went back to the days of training to become a jumper. *Boy, was I young*, he thought. *I actually enjoyed learning how to be a 'hunter'. When I arrived at the new farm where my new owner lived, I saw a field with all white fences around it. Then, there were a number of short fences of all different types of fences in the middle of the field. When I looked closer there was a riding ring around the inside of the fencing and the short fences were all in middle of the pasture, in the grassy area. I wondered what they were for.*

Well, I soon found out that the short fences were for me to jump. No more jumping in and out of the fields. I also learned that my rider used a different kind of saddle than the ones the jockeys used at the racing stable where I was born. First, I had to get used to the new saddle and the weight of the riders. The riders usually weighed more than the jockeys. Then, I got to show them what I could do going over those fences in the middle of the field. My rider called them "jumps".

Every day, we'd go into the field with the jumps and I would learn more and more about how to take jumps. We'd take many of them each time we went in the 'ring', as they called it. I learned that I had to take a certain number of strides between each different jump. I felt myself getting stronger and stronger in the hind quarters. Actually, I got a lot of compliments during my training. I was sure this was what I was meant to do.

One late spring day, my trainer told me that in a few days we'd being going to a Horse Show. He explained that my owner would be riding me in a ring just like the one I'd trained in but the jumps, those short sections of different kinds of fences, would be arranged differently. 'Okay', I thought, 'I can handle that'.

That was the beginning of my career as a hunter. Taking jumps inside the ring was called Stadium Jumping. Then we'd gallop through a course in the woods and in meadows with lots of different things to jump, like hedges or steams. That was called a Cross Country course and was always fun but could be really tiring. Then I learned to be even more attuned to my rider in a skill called Dressage. Boy, you really had to pay attention. When you were doing Dressage, you had to know exactly what your rider wanted you to do. I knew because my rider would give me signals that I could feel but no one else could really see. And I was good at it as I learned not to let my mind wander. In the Dressage ring, I really paid close attention to my rider. Each move had to be very precise and they weren't easy moves but really fun to get just right.

I knew I was good because they kept pinning blue ribbons on me and my rider, who was by now usually the same gentleman. After I'd get my blue ribbon my rider would pet me on the neck. Then, we'd proudly do a couple of circles around the ring before he'd take me back to the stable. I have to admit I got a little cocky because I knew how good I was at being a hunter. I had won so many blue ribbons and my owner had gotten so many shiny pieces of silver, called trophies, that I thought I was unbeatable. I'd hear the trainer and my owner talking and planning for the next horse shows we'd go to. Then many years later I heard a new word I'd not heard before.

What was an Olympics? I wondered if this was something new. My rider was all excited and then I noticed my training became more and more difficult. By this time, I was beginning *to feel all of the hard work. The years had gone by faster than I would have dreamed but I still had a lot of jumps in me.*

The groom and my trainer used to watch a game they called football in the tack room. I could just see the TV from my stall. Men were playing a game that seemed like some kind of battle and they'd run into each other and crash to the ground. I often thought they must hurt all over after the game was over. That was how I was feeling more and more after a hard work-out.

It wasn't long before it was clear to me that the Olympics were very important. I understood that we were going someplace to try out for them as the men kept talking about the Olympic Trials. I knew we had won lots of blue ribbons at the Grand Prix Shows but didn't understand this Olympic thing. Oh well, I had learned to "go with the flow," as the grooms called it.

Early one morning they put me in my trailer, which I was accustomed to riding in, and off we went for what turned out to be a very long ride. In fact, it took us two days and nights to get where we were going. We stopped often along the way, and the groom would take me out of my trailer and we'd walk around. That helped me not get stiff from riding so long. They'd feed and water me in my trailer and off we'd go again. We arrived early one morning, and my owner was already there. He led me out of the trailer and looked me over, checking my feet and legs and talking to a group of other men who were there. I lifted my head high and put both ears forward to look my very best. They were clearly impressed.

My owner led me to this huge stable and then to what was to be my stall while we were there. 'Nice digs', I thought. I'd heard the groom say that earlier. Well, it was a terrific stable but when you've seen one stall you've seen them all. Anyway, we were here, and I was glad to get out of that trailer.

A little while later, the trainer came to get me and we had our regular workout. I will have to say that the grounds around the stable and the jumping ring were something special. There were bushes and flowers and everything was perfect, like in some of these posters the guys hang up in the tack room. It was clear to me that we were at someplace unusual.

Still pondering back to those surroundings at the Trials, Darby drifted off to sleep, standing in his HOPE stable. He liked remembering his former life as each time he'd remember something that would help him do the work he now had here at HOPE. *Horses Helping People* he often thought. *I had always assumed that was my job when I was a jumping horse.* People seemed to want him to perform with them but that had not been as satisfying to him as this work was at HOPE. Here he could actually see the need people had for him. Blue ribbons were nice, but this was better.

When he woke up the next morning, he remembered he had two patients today. Both little girls that seemed to have some issues that made it hard for them to communicate with other people. He'd overheard one of their parents use the word Autism. Autism, must be what they call the problem these patients had. Whatever they called it, Darby knew what he needed to do. This was a day to be very attentive and careful. With an autism patient, Darby had to watch intently and move slowly. Sometimes, he'd actually get one of these little girls to look him in the eye but that was usually after they had been coming to HOPE for many weeks. Working with the children was very different from working with the men from Honor House.

His first patient was Emma, and she'd been coming to HOPE for nearly two months. She'd become comfortable enough, at HOPE, to now come running to see Darby when she arrived at the barn. Out of the corner of his eyes, Darby saw Emma coming into the stable. Her mother was always close behind. He stretched his neck down to position his nose where Emma could reach him with a quick pat.

It had been a good day and both of Darby's patients had advanced to riding in the ring. They both loved it and would say goodbye to Darby before they left. That sounds like a little thing but for these two young girls, it was really important that they had made a connection with the big horse.

After a bath and his dinner, Darby allowed his mind to go back to his glory days as a jumper. At his age, memories were an important part of his life. He knew that tomorrow was the day that Johnny would be coming to HOPE, and he felt there was something in his past that would help him to truly understand and help Johnny. He was not just daydreaming but trying to find something that could help him to understand Johnny better. *I've never been to war*, Darby wondered, *how can I understand what Johnny has been through and where he goes in his mind*. It was late and Darby began to dose off to sleep and dream.

"Okay Darby," his owner said as he had approached him the first morning of the Olympic Trials. "Let's win this boy. I know we can do it and then…well, if we win this then we can go to the big battle, the Olympics, after a lot more training that is."

Darby's head snapped up in his stall at HOPE. His ears immediately were at attention. He remembered those words and hadn't really understood them at the time but now that word had become very familiar to him. He'd heard some of the veterans who came to HOPE talk about the battles they'd fought in. Then they'd say, how much they hated war. He had to think hard about how all of this was related. He always listened to everything that was said, in the barn or anywhere. He'd heard the volunteers talking about something called PTSD and that the veterans that came here suffered from it. He wondered, if that was some kind of injury they got when they were in a battle. He'd been in a battle and maybe the Olympic Trials were like a war, three days of battles. They were very hard days and there would be losers and winners. Just the word war made him shiver. *It must be something really bad*, he thought. *What have I experienced that will help me understand what has happened to Johnny?*

Fully awake now, he let his mind wander back to Olympic Trials. The first morning there, he had his breakfast, a groom came to lead him out of his stall, and they walked around the grounds. Lots of other trailers were parked in a special place provided for them. There were lots of other horses walking around and some were arriving in their trailers, some of which were large and very fancy looking. This wasn't unusual for a Grand Prix Show but there was something special about this place and Darby couldn't figure it out. *What are these Olympics*, he wondered.

Later, after a couple of hours in his stall, his owner came by and rubbed his nose and then his forehead. "This is a big day boy. We need to do a workout this morning and get used to the course." Darby had learned that the course was: where and how the jumps were set up in the ring and determined which jumps they'd take and in what order.

Darby remembered that he'd whinnied and had shaken his head up and down as if to say, "Okay, I've got it Chief." He liked to think of his owner as the Chief. He was trying to say, "Let's do this thing". Darby had nothing if not confidence in his ability in the jumping ring.

"We have three days of work to do Darby," his owner said.

Oh, thought Darby, *we're at what I've heard them call a 'three day event'.* Darby always liked the day when they did what was called Cross Country as he got to gallop across fields, jump fences, and creeks. It wasn't actually a race but you did need to do this Cross Country in what was considered 'very good time'. Darby knew that meant 'as fast as possible'. Strangely, while Darby was not fast enough to be a race horse he was fast enough to perform very well in the Cross Country competition. He attributed that to his jumping skills. As he was remembering galloping across those beautiful fields that day, he drifted off to sleep again.

He wakened the next morning just after the sun had come up over HOPE. It was a Wednesday and that meant that Johnny would be there in the afternoon. His morning patient was a little girl who had braces on both of her legs. Darby had to be careful, especially when she led him out of the barn. As walking for her was very difficult. He often thought, how strange it must look for this little girl with her legs moving with leather and metal on them leading him, a very big horse. He kept his head down to make her grip on the lead closer to where her hand was and so she wouldn't have to stretch up to keep her hand only a few inches from his halter. He needed to be very alert when she was with him. His objective was to help her feel confident that she could lead and control this big horse. She needed confidence that she could be normal, even with her legs being in those braces. The morning went well and after his morning patient left HOPE, one of the volunteers took Darby to the big pasture. There he could exercise, run, and then graze on the good green grass. It felt good to exercise and burn up some energy before his afternoon patient arrived.

Darby saw the white car arrive a couple of hours later. He recognized that this was the car from Honor House. He knew today was going to be very important, as he needed to get Johnny to talk to him more about why he was here. Darby knew that Johnny was experiencing a very deep sadness. Something terrible must have happened to make a man who had been a physician want nothing to do with his ability to help people any more.

Darby had been thinking of how he could help Johnny and hadn't noticed that his patient was actually standing beside the pasture gate with a lead. Once he saw him, Darby galloped over to the gate and his day with Johnny began.

"Hi boy," said Johnny. "I'm glad to see you. They told me we were going to do some new things today. I'm ready. Are you?"

Darby whinnied in answer. *Ready*, he thought. *I've been waiting to see you. Now let's get started.* As he was thinking this, he let Johnny hook the lead to his halter and he walked around the gate and began his day with his patient. He needed to let Johnny know that he'd missed him and was glad to see him, so Darby placed his head on Johnny's shoulder.

"Thanks Darby," Johnny said. "I've missed you too. It's been a hard week and life seems all black and terrible." Then Johnny looked down to the ground and said, "What am I doing? I'm talking to a dumb animal like he was my psychiatrist."

When Darby heard the "dumb animal" characterization of himself, he jerked the lead from Johnny's hand and took off at a gallop, jumping pasture fences, all to get away from this man who he had cared so much about and who thought of him as a 'dumb animal'. After jumping into the pasture farthest from the stable, Darby stopped and looked back at Johnny who was now a long way away and looked very small. *Whoa,* thought Darby, *let's don't judge him too harshly. We all knew he had problems or he wouldn't be here. That was anger at something in his life and I was just the closest one to strike out and hurt. This isn't over and maybe I did the right thing. Let's see what he does next.* Then, Darby raised his head and put his ears back and stood and waited.

Sure enough, Johnny was walking toward him and opening and closing gates to get to the pasture where Darby stood waiting. Ears still back, when Johnny came close, Darby took several steps back as if to say, "I'm not sure I want anything to do with you."

Still walking toward him, Johnny reached out his hand and said, "Darby, I'm sorry. I'm really sorry." Darby stopped backing up but kept his ears back, trying to look angry. "You understood what I said didn't you boy?" Johnny asked as he put his hand out toward Darby. "I didn't know you understood what people said and I did say something terrible. Clearly, there is nothing dumb about you. I'm the dumb one. I just didn't know how really smart you are".

At that, Darby relaxed his ears and took two steps toward Johnny as if to say, "I hear you but I'm not sure I believe you." There was no show of affection from Darby, only an offer to listen.

"Darby," said Johnny. "Help me to understand what you understand. I guess because you can't talk we humans forget that you can listen, and you can learn what we are saying. You clearly knew what I said a few moments ago." At that Darby shook his head up and down in a clear 'yes' motion. "You do understand," said Johnny as he came to Darby and put his arms around Darby's neck. He then whispered in Darby's left ear, "You may be the only friend I have that can listen to my terrible thoughts. I need a friend Darby. I need someone who can listen to me and not judge me. Can you do that?"

Darby slowly moved his head up and down rubbing against Johnny's cheek. The two stood together in the pasture for a few more moments, just quietly communicating as Johnny rubbed Darby's neck. As they stood there, one of the volunteers came running through the pastures to reach them.

"Is everything okay out here?" she asked. "Darby, what were you doing jumping those fences? Johnny, are you okay?" She pelted out questions so fast that they ran together. Then she stopped seeing the horse and his patient, obviously having a moment of friendship. "Everything's okay, right?" she asked. "I guess Darby just had to show you what an amazing jumper he is. Right Darby?"

Darby shook his head to say, "Yes," and Johnny quietly said, "Isn't he something? Boy, this horse can jump." At that Johnny, who had carried the lead with him into the pasture, then dropped it when he realized that Darby could understand everything he said. As the volunteer left, Johnny reached down and picked it up and connected it to Darby's halter. "Come on boy, we have somethings to do and I guess the fun has to wait a while. Back to work", Johnny said in an apologetic voice.

As they walked back to the stable, Darby was thinking about what Johnny had said. *I understand better now, he's angry. That's why he said those things. He's just angry but what about? What has hurt Johnny so much that he carries around so much anger? I've got to find out and get him to talk about it and now that he knows I understand what he's saying, maybe we can get him to tell me about it. From what he said,* Darby thought, *he's tried talking to people but they seemed to judge him. I think he knows that I won't. I can just listen and understand what is making him so angry. Then maybe he can find his way back to his life.*

Chapter 7

Now that Darby and Johnny understood each other, Johnny felt free to talk to Darby and Darby would listen and understand. It was the breakthrough that Darby needed to be able to help Johnny. The weeks went by and each week Johnny would come and he and Darby would walk the pastures. Johnny would tell Darby things that happened, which made him unable to cope with going back to the life he'd lived before the War.

"They call it PTSD, Darby," Johnny said one afternoon as they were walking together. "The P stands for Post, which means after. The T is for Traumatic. The best way I can define that is something that happens which is so terrible that it frightens your brain. It's like your brain being damaged by something you see or are a part of. Darby, I saw so much Trauma. I can never explain how bad it was," Johnny said as tears flowed out of his eyes, rolling down his face.

Darby laid his head on Johnny's shoulder and leaned his head against Johnny cheek. Darby thought to himself, *how can I comfort him? What he sees in his mind when he remembers must be awful. After all, before he went to War he was an Emergency Room Doctor. They've seen many people hurt. I've heard the grooms and trainer in my old stable talk about going to the Emergency Room when one of them got really badly hurt.* He pulled his head up and looked in Johnny's eyes. It was like he wasn't there but was looking far away and not even aware that Darby was there. *I have to get his attention again,* Darby thought. *I've got to bring him back here with me. Just by explaining it to me, he wandered back to those terrible places.*

Darby, with his right hoof, touched Johnny's leg and then pawed the ground three times. Johnny's head jerked and looked at him once he felt Darby's hoof on his leg. "Hay Darby, why did you do that?" Johnny asked. "Wait a minute, you were trying to get my attention, weren't you? I'm sorry Darby, I guess I went back there. You knew that didn't you, boy?" Johnny asked Darby and expected an answer.

Darby immediately shook his head in an up and down motion. "Okay boy, we've got to get this communication thing really working," said Johnny. I know we've got yes and no down when you move your head, but I'd prefer you not hit me when I drift off in my mind. Why don't you just paw the ground and if I don't get it, then touch my leg. Does that work for you?"

Darby shook his head as if saying, 'Yes'. Johnny then stood very still and Darby knew he was thinking.

"Okay Darby, I know you have to listen to all of my demons when I go into those long speeches about all that is wrong with my life and how I feel about why I just can't go back to being a doctor. When I get out of control, can you use your nose to get my attention?"

At that question, Darby put his nose on Johnny's chest and drew it up under Johnny's chin. "Wow," Johnny said as he jumped in surprise. "That'll get my attention." Johnny got very quiet for a minute and then actually smiled. That was something Darby hadn't seen before.

"Darby, we can actually talk. You understand and can give me the information that I need and when I need it. This is amazing my friend and you are my friend." Johnny reached up and hugged Darby's neck. This was a real hug and something that had never happened before. The two stood there for a long time as Johnny took in the importance of this. He thought of all the doctors he'd seen, all the other people and medicine that they had given him to take. Yet, he still suffered from PTSD. Maybe he always would but now he could talk to someone who really cared for him, wouldn't ever judge him or argue with him. Darby was someone who would listen and get his attention when he needed to remember where he was and what he was doing. Somehow Johnny knew that he might have hope again.

Johnny never finished explaining PTSD to Darby but the big horse seemed to understand that it was bad and really hurt the people who suffered with it. Somewhere in his mind Darby thought that maybe he understood what Trauma was.

"It was a great day Darby", Johnny said just before Bryan from Honor House came to tell him it was time to leave. "It has to be our little secret, boy. No one would believe how well we can talk but I am so grateful. Strange," Johnny said slowly. "That's the first time I've been grateful for anything for a long time. Thanks Buddy," he said as he ran his hand down Darby's neck.

That night Darby thought more about the word 'trauma'. As he stood in his stall Darby's mind went back to the Olympic Trials. He thought he knew what trauma was. He would think about this PTSD more and try to understand it better.

As the weeks went by, Johnny learned to really ride Darby and they would walk all over the grounds. Some days they could go down a riding path that had been created for those patients that had good riding skills. Johnny was becoming a good rider, with Darby's help, of course.

Johnny was a veteran, as were all of the men that lived at Honor House. Darby knew that a veteran was someone who had fought in a War. Well, not all of them had actually been in a War but they had all served in the Military. You see, the staff at HOPE didn't know it but they often had the television on in the tack room and Darby always listened when the news came on. He learned a great deal about people from the news. While he didn't know a lot about war, he knew it wasn't good and that many people would get hurt or some might even die in a war. He knew that war was the reason some people would be so disturbed that they couldn't live the same lives they had lived before they went to war. They had to learn to live all over again.

Johnny talked about the War in Iraq. Darby didn't know what Iraq was or where it was, but he knew it was far away, in another land and it had a lot of sand. Darby knew about sand because they'd used it at HOPE when they were building things and he knew it felt soft and moved under his feet. He'd stepped on a sand pile once and he sank into the sand. That was not fun. So, drawing on that experience, Darby could imagine what a sandy land was like. Johnny had told him that in Iraq they didn't have dirt like we had but the land was covered with sand.

Johnny had been a doctor in Iraq and his patients had been the people who were hurt in the war. He'd told Darby about how good it felt to save a man who was badly injured. He also told Darby how terrible it was when he couldn't save someone. Darby knew that this was where much of the anger came from and why Johnny didn't want to be a doctor again. You see, Darby understood that kind of loss because he'd had a friend who became very sick when he was in the hunter stable. Horses make friends easily but this horse, his name was Woody and he was Darby's best friend. He was big and strong and could jump even better than Darby. Darby had learned a great deal just watching his friend jumping a course.

One night his friend, who lived in the stall beside Darby's, laid down and couldn't get up. The groom had gotten the trainer and soon the Vet, who Darby understood was a doctor for animals. The Vet came and went in his friend's stall. Then, the trainer and the Vet came outside of Woody's stall and talked. They didn't seem to know that Darby could understand them. The Vet told the trainer that Woody was very sick and would likely not live through the night. Darby knew that meant that his friend was dying. He would never be there beside Darby anymore. The Vet said he had given Woody something for the pain he was in, so he would sleep. Maybe by morning they would know more, only Woody didn't live until morning.

Darby was taken out of his stall in the morning but when he left he saw that Woody was sleeping very still on the floor of his stall. When Darby came back to his stall, Woody was gone and he would never see him again. Darby guessed that was what it meant to die, to go away from everyone and never come back. He had been sad and then he had been angry that no one had told him where Woody had gone. Maybe that's how Johnny feels about the soldiers he couldn't save, angry that they are gone and he couldn't keep them from going away.

As the weather became cooler Johnny and Darby would spend the Wednesdays together and Johnny seemed less angry, more willing to joke and laugh. He'd told Darby about so many things that had made him angry and then little by little he'd begin to talk about things he'd like to do with his life. He'd never been married but seemed to want to be. He knew he could never face being a doctor again but talked about other things he might like to do with this life. Some days he even seemed hopeful. Those were the good days when Darby felt like he'd been able to really help Johnny. Some days Johnny would not be cheerful and Darby would work extra hard to get him to talk.

Johnny never missed a Wednesday at HOPE and Darby, while he loved all of his other patients, he particularly looked forward to Johnny's days there. Darby felt that Johnny was his star patient, the one for whom he had been able to do the most. Johnny had become his best friend, if people can be a horse's best friend.

Chapter 8

One night as he stood in his stall, Darby began to think back about how he came to be at HOPE. It was a particularly cold night and Darby had his blanket on. He could still feel the cold. He knew that the best way to deal with cold was not to think about it. It reminded him of the cold the last night he was at the Olympic Trials. He'd been cold that night too. Trying to forget about the cold, something unusual in Florida, he let his mind wander back to his days at the Olympic Trials.

Darby remembered feeling really good after the Cross Country race. He'd been given a blue ribbon that day. The next day was the Dressage class. It was more like a demonstration by one horse at a time. There were a number of specific moves that the rider could guide the horse to perform using only his/her legs to give the horse signals. A Judge would call out the movement she or he wanted to see the horse and rider perform. It was kind of like dancing with the rider as the leader. Darby had loved to show off in the Dressage performance. Another day and another Blue Ribbon.

The Chief was really excited. Two days and they'd won the two Blue Ribbons. He rubbed Darby down himself, talking to him all of the time. Darby was happy about it because the grooms usually did his baths and rub downs. The Chief, his owner, almost never spent time with him until he mounted to go into the show ring. Darby didn't feel like he really knew the man but performed at his very best for him. Besides, Darby had always liked to perform. He did recognize that it is now more tiring than it used to be. *After all*, Darby thought, *I am getting up in years*.

Darby remembered that he'd heard one of the grooms talk about the fact that Darby was 12-years-old. That's not really old for a horse, but just like people, as horses grow older, sometimes they start to hurt after hard exercise. As Darby stood, feeling the cold a bit, he was aware that his hind quarters were a little stiff. He walked around his stall to try to work out the stiffness and to get a little warmer.

The next day was the stadium jumping competition. It was the final day of the first round of the Trials. Darby listened intently as the grooms talked among themselves while they cleaned his saddle and braided his mane and tail. He'd always wondered why he had to be all braided up to go in a ring and show how well he could jump. *Oh well*, he thought, *whatever it takes to keep the Chief happy*. As he had walked into the aisle of the stable to stand for the braiding, he felt that stiffness again. *Gotta move*, he thought. *Gotta work it out*.

He remembered that feeling as he stood in his stall at HOPE. He remembered that the grooms finished braiding and put on his saddle and bridal almost immediately and then leading him out to where the Chief was standing.

"Morning, Darby," said the Chief. "We're first up this morning so let's go to the workout ring and get you warmed up."

The Chief mounted Darby and guided him to the ring where he'd work out. Sure enough, a little walking and Darby's hind quarters felt better. He took a few jumps and was beginning to feel good when the groom said, "It's time to go in the ring," and the Chief guided Darby to the main show ring.

Here we go, thought Darby as he looked around the field going from a lazy trot to a full cantor before getting to the first jump. Darby knew it was time to concentrate on what he had to do now. It was a long course with every different kind of jump Darby had ever seen, ten jumps. They'd do the exterior jumps and then go to the interior jumps which included two sets of jumps that only allowed for one stride between the jumps. The Grooms called those sets of jumps, 'in and outs'. They were the hardest.

The first set was perfect, then they sailed over the second set. *Now just two more jumps,* thought Darby. *I've got this.* The next to last jump looked like a rock wall but Darby knew it was just wood painted that way. He jumped it and then had to take a curve to approach the last jump. It was a jump with three poles and pretty standard. As he approached the jump, Darby felt something wasn't quite right but he cantered on and began his lunge from his hind legs but there was no strength. His hind legs failed him, and he crashed into the jump and the Chief was thrown over the jump and on to the ground.

Suddenly, there was lots of confusion in that ring. Darby, with no rider on his back, began to back up to get out of the way as people came running to help the Chief. A groom ran over and took Darby's reins to lead him away from the ring. As they started to walk Darby realized that his hind quarters were really hurting again. But he tried to ignore the pain as he tried to make sense out of what happened.

"You okay, boy?" asked the groom as they walked back to the stable. Darby knew the groom didn't really expect an answer and he also realized that every step was painful and he had to be lame. Darby threw his head around to try and see what had happened to the Chief. Then Darby thought, *What if I've really hurt him? What if he's really injured?* At that very moment he saw the Chief up and walking around. *He looks okay,* thought Darby. *Thank goodness, he looks okay.*

Suddenly, Darby realized he'd been dreaming and was standing in his stall at HOPE. He remembered his dream, a dream of the worst day of his life. He'd failed. He'd caused the Chief to lose the jumping competition. He'd heard the grooms say that because of the fall, the Chief and Darby would not have a chance to go to the Olympics. Whatever they were, Darby knew they were very important to the Chief and that had made them very important to Darby.

Darby wondered why all of this was coming back to him now. That was two years ago but then he remembered that the day he fell, the day he disappointed his owner was the beginning of the events that brought him to HOPE. It had truly been the terrible day that changed his life. He'd failed. He'd failed the Chief, the trainer, the grooms and he guessed he'd failed himself. Suddenly, Darby had realized his glory days in the ring were over.

Darby saw those next few days pass through his mind. Oh, they'd had a Veterinarian look him over. Darby heard the Vet say, "He's just getting older and clearly has arthritis in his hind quarters. He's just not going to be a dependable hunter anymore."

Darby remembered becoming very depressed as he realized that if he couldn't be a hunter and couldn't be a race horse, there was no reason for him to go on. While the Vet had given him a shot to help with the pain, it couldn't help the pain he felt in his heart and in his brain. He remembered, feeling useless and wondered what kind of future he could have. Then he heard the Vet say, "His hind quarters are clearly inflamed and if you look, you'll see they are slightly swollen. I don't know how he jumped as much as he did of that course at the Trials. Let the meds help and do keep him moving. The worst thing would be for him to not keep moving. In a few days and with some exercise each day, he may actually be able to jump again but never at this level and no more Three-Day Eventing." The Chief walked over and patted Darby's neck.

"Well guy, I guess I understand what happened. Thank God neither one of us were hurt. It was pretty traumatic, wasn't it?" Those words didn't make Darby feel any better but the Chief seemed to be sincere. It had been just awful, probably the worst thing he could think of. Darby wasn't sure what the word traumatic meant but if it meant scary and terrible, then he understood.

As they loaded him in the trailer for the long drive back to his home stable, Darby remembered just wanting to die. He thought he had no reason to go on living. Like his friend Woodie, he'd like to just go away and never come back.

Darby kept running the moments as he crashed into the jump over in his brain and then remembered the horror of it. What if he'd killed his owner or he'd broken a leg and had to have been put down? *What if, what if, what if,* he kept thinking but he didn't die. He had to go on living and being useless. With that thought and remembering how awful the depression felt, Darby went back to sleep in his stall at HOPE.

The next morning as Darby was eating his oats, he remembered the word 'traumatic' from his dreams the night before. He raised his head from the oats bucket. It was like a flash of understanding. The word 'traumatic' came blasting into his mind. When he fell, the Chief called it traumatic. He wondered if that is the same as the word 'traumatic' like in PTSD. 'Post-Traumatic Stress Syndrome' was what it stood for. He'd heard Terry say those words. He knew what stress was, as some of the children that came there would get scared at first. He heard a parent once say that her daughter would get very stressed before they would come to HOPE. He thought she meant a form of frightened.

Could that be what has happened to Johnny? He had a terrible experience or maybe a lot of terrible experiences? Could that be why he is so depressed and angry and always so on edge with him? Darby kept asking himself questions, all in an attempt to understand what many of the veterans felt that came to HOPE.

Well, today is Wednesday, thought Darby, *so Johnny will be here and somehow, I have to let him know I understand, that I've been there too. Let's see*, Darby thought, *maybe I can turn the tables on him. I know what it is like to feel awful after a traumatic experience. I know what I understand is nothing like as bad as Johnny lived through but at least I have some way of understanding him better. I wonder how he will take it if I'm the one that is sad and depressed today.* Then Darby smiled inside remembering what it was to put on a show. After all, that's what a hunter who is a show horse does.

Then, Darby had to think back and remember how it was to be sad and angry because of the 'traumatic' event, of falling into the jump and nearly killing the Chief. He remembered he didn't eat because food tasted awful. He didn't want to leave his stall, but they made him walk and he didn't have the energy to walk very far. He'd actually tried to kick a groom who wanted him to trot in order not to stiffen up. How can he show Johnny that he understands and has also suffered with some PTSD? Darby knew what he'd been through wasn't as awful as war or the awful things Johnny had to have suffered but he did understand him better now.

Darby thought that Johnny was some better now but there were still those days when he was hard to reach and didn't want to communicate with Darby. *Somehow*, Darby thought *I've got to be able to get through to him at those times.*

Johnny arrived a little early that day only to find Darby standing in the back of his stall, head down, and ears back. "Hey Darby," Johnny said as he opened the stall door. Darby didn't move and didn't look up.

"What's wrong Darby," Johnny asked as he walked over to the horse that hadn't moved. Johnny had always seen Darby waiting in the front of his stall with his head and neck extended out into the aisle as if to say 'Welcome' when Johnny came into the stable. "You sick, Darby?" Johnny asked as he rubbed his hand down Darby's face as if to take his temperature. "Maybe you just need to get out of the stall. Let's take a walk, boy," Johnny said as he left the stall to go and get a lead.

As Johnny came to him to attach the lead Darby, the big horse kept thinking of how he was going to get Johnny to understand. He needed Johnny to know that he'd had a traumatic event too and he knew how it felt. *That's a big job*, thought Darby. *Oh, if I could only talk and share it with him. Well, now I've got to see how good I am at remembering, how it felt and how I acted.* As Johnny started walking out of Darby's stall, Darby didn't move.

"Come on, boy. Let's take a walk. The sun is out and it's a warm day. It was kind of cold last night," Johnny coaxed Darby. Darby didn't move and wouldn't look at Johnny, keeping his head down near the floor of his stall.

Not understanding what was wrong with Darby, Johnny reached in his pocket and pulled out an apple. "Look here Darby, I've brought you your apple," he said.

Darby almost got really angry. *He thinks he can bribe me to be happy*, Darby thought, remembering how the grooms at his old stable would try and bribe him to leave his stall. It's more than something an apple can cure, Darby remembered. He actually felt the anger come back that he'd felt after his accident. Then he remembered, *it wasn't an accident. It was me. I couldn't jump anymore, not like I once could. It was my fault, all my fault*, he thought to himself feeling the anger overtake him again.

Johnny stood there still trying to coax Darby out of his stall. Suddenly, Johnny saw what Darby was feeling. It looked familiar and he could feel that Darby was really depressed. He disconnected the lead and left the stall saying, "I'll be back in a few minutes, Darby."

Darby watched him leave and wondered what Johnny was going to do. *Well, I've tried to remind him of how he is feeling*, he thought. *He left here with something in mind*, Darby thought as Johnny went looking for the man he knew to be the Executive Director of HOPE.

"Terry, can I talk to you a minute," Johnny called out as he nearly bumped into Terry. They had both been coming around the same corner of the stable but walking in different directions. "Terry, there's something wrong with Darby and I don't think it's physical. He seems depressed," Johnny said. "What can you tell me about Darby? Did anything happen to him since I was here? How long has he been at HOPE? How old is Darby and do you know what's happened to him?" Johnny kept firing questions at Terry. Suddenly, he stopped, realizing that he needed to give the poor man time to answer.

"Johnny, let's walk over here," Terry said as he took Johnny by the elbow and led him farther away from the stable. "Darby came here from a big-time hunter stable where he'd been a major show jumping horse. He even went so far as the Olympic Trials for hunters and riders."

Before Terry could finish, Johnny asked, "How did he end up here?"

"Well," said Terry, "after winning the first two days of a Three-Day Eventing competition at the Olympic Trials, he crashed into the last jump in the Stadium Jumping Competition. He and his rider were really lucky, neither was injured but the Vet who examined Darby found that he'd developed arthritis in his hind quarters and by the end of three grueling days of performing, the arthritis was really painful. He just hadn't had the strength to take that last jump. It was amazing that he'd jumped the entire course perfectly, until he came to that last jump." Terry explained.

"What happened to him after that?" asked Johnny.

"Well," said Terry, "Darby became despondent after the crash. He became difficult for his grooms to exercise, even after the painfulness was taken care of by medications. He'd just stand in his stall, his head down, unwilling to eat or react to anyone. Why do you ask?"

"Boy, do I know how he felt," Johnny said before he realized that Terry was listening.

"You asked how he got here," Terry said. "He was given to us to see if our therapy training could begin to bring him out of it. Darby could never be a show jumper again. He responded to the training to become a therapy horse." Terry stopped talking and looked at Johnny seeing sincere concern for the horse. "You know Darby is the smartest horse I've ever seen. Does that help you?" Terry asked.

"It sure does," said Johnny. "It sure does," he said as he turned to walk back to the stable. "And thanks. Thanks a lot," he called back to Terry. Johnny smiled as he realized what was happening. *That rascal is giving me a dose of my own medicine. So, Darby knows what it is like to feel like he's lost everything. He lost his home too and had to start his life all over again. Just like me,* Johnny thought. *The bad thing is that he's done a better job of it than I have. Terry was right, Darby's smart, really smart. He's giving me what I've been giving him*, Johnny thought as he entered the stable.

"Okay, snap out of it," Johnny said as he entered Darby's stall. "You rascal, you were giving me a dose of my own medicine. Have I been this difficult? I know that you know what I've been going through and this little act was to show me that you'd been where I am now. Well, you did it," Johnny whispered in Darby's ear. "I've got to find my way out just like you did. Thanks boy, now let's go outside and have some fun."

Chapter 9

Darby was really feeling good. The sun was shining. It was a nearly perfect 75 degrees and Johnny seemed actually happy for the first time since Darby had known him. Julie, the volunteer, asked Johnny if he was going to ride today. It would be the first time that Johnny had actually ridden Darby on the long trails. Darby shook his head as if saying, 'Yes,' after Johnny had asked him if he thought he was ready.

Julie showed Johnny again how to put on Darby's saddle and bridle himself. The groom had always done it for him before. He caught on quickly and soon he was ready to mount Darby and go for a ride. Darby had never seen Johnny so chatty with Julie. He had taken instructions and asked questions about putting the saddle on and was particularly interested in cinching the girth. Darby wondered to himself why they called it cinching the girth when it was just buckling the belly strap that kept the saddle in place on his back. *Oh well*, thought Darby, *I guess riders have their own language.*

As Johnny mounted Darby and Julie showed him again how to hold the reins and how to use them to guide Darby, the big horse whinnied as loudly as Johnny had ever heard him. "I think that was Darby's way of saying that he knows where he's going," said Johnny. "And he probably does. He knows a lot of things."

Darby was elated at all that had happened that day and would have loved to run and jump for joy, but he knew that Johnny was not that skilled a rider and he had to be well mannered. He could run and play in the pasture after Johnny had gone back to Honor House. *Now*, Darby thought, *let's give Johnny a ride that he will really enjoy and be happy about*. Johnny being happy was a new thought for Darby as he'd just never seen it before.

As he was riding Darby, the sun was warm on his face, Johnny smiled, thinking to himself. *I'd forgotten how good it felt to be happy, to enjoy something and to have a friend*. He reached down and patted Darby's neck, "You are my very good friend Darby and I will never forget what you have taught me."

At that, Darby whinnied, swished his tail from side to side and began a slow trot. He knew he should just walk as this was Johnny's first trail ride, but he just couldn't contain himself or his happiness. Johnny didn't mind and began to bounce in the saddle in perfect time to Darby's trot.

Before Johnny left that afternoon, he'd ridden and then bathed Darby, chatting constantly about what a good time he'd had riding and how good he'd felt. Once he'd dried Darby with a scraper and then a towel, he walked Darby to his stall. Darby walked over to get a drink of water.

"Hey boy," called Johnny, "didn't you forget something?" Darby turned and walked over to Johnny who was standing outside the stall with a big, red apple in his hand. "Today, I can honestly say you've earned this. In fact, you've earned so much more. Darby, no human being could ever have done as much for me as you did today. You shared your deepest feelings and pain with me to help me see myself and that I can come back. I can feel good again. Darby, you showed me that there can be a good life, a productive life after all the hurt and sadness." As he handed the apple to Darby with one hand, he reached up hugged his neck with the other.

As Darby took the apple in his mouth, he leaned into Johnny's hug. He had wished he could talk and say, *I love you too* but laying his head against Johnny's neck was about the best he could do. *He finally understands*, thought Darby. *Now we are on our way*. There's more work to do but this was the really big break-through that Darby had hoped to make with Johnny. He now remembered that he could be happy. Darby knew that this feeling was the key to Johnny getting well.

"See you next week, my friend," said Johnny as he turned to go to the car and then back to Honor House. "It was a very good day," he called back to anyone who was listening. Darby heard him as he crunched his apple. Boy, it did taste good and he felt it was a proper reward for such a good day.

Terry, who was in charge at HOPE, walked over to Darby's stall. "I don't know what happened today," he said, "but that's the first time I've ever seen Johnny smile. Somehow, I think this was a very significant day for him and Darby," he paused as if to think of the right words. "Darby, you did something special today. I don't pretend to understand what you did but whatever it was, you performed a miracle." Terry reached up to pet Darby. "Bryan had told me that Johnny was the worst case of PTSD they'd ever seen and he had little hope that we could help him. But if there are more days like today," he said as he looked Darby right in the eyes. "Darby, you may have just saved a life today."

Chapter 10

The rest of that week Darby was very engaged with each of his patients. He concentrated on every patient's individual needs and tried to communicate with each of them. One young man seemed to understand and respond. This young man responded very slowly but any response was something new. Darby took pleasure in every small success now. Most of all he was looking forward to Wednesday afternoon when the white car from Honor House would pull into the parking area.

This next Wednesday in early December, it was really chilly. Darby just thought it was just cold. That didn't happen often in Florida where HOPE was located but once in a while the temperature would dip. On those days Darby loved to get out of his stall and run in the pastures. It would warm him up and make him feel good but since Johnny was coming he'd wait in his stall with his blanket on. *After the great day they'd had the previous week, today should be easy to take the next step in Johnny's recovery*, thought Darby.

It was time for Johnny to come and the white car parked in the lot beside the road. Darby could just barely see the parking lot from his stall but if he stood up in the very front of his stall and leaned his neck out as far as possible he could see the white car. Bryan from Honor House got out as did two other men but Johnny wasn't with them. Darby started to worry that maybe Johnny was sick or had been hurt. That happened sometimes to his patients and they'd miss a week of their therapy at HOPE. Darby worried about Johnny and no one told him why Johnny wasn't there. One of the volunteers just took Darby out to the pasture, removing his blanket so he could get some exercise. Running in the pasture did make

Darby warmer but the entire time he was wondering where Johnny might be and what could be wrong.

Week after week went by and Johnny didn't come back. Darby never stopped looking for him. Christmas came and went. The stable was always decorated for Christmas and while Darby didn't understand what Christmas was all about, he knew it was a special time for humans. He continued to go about his work but he never stopped wondering about Johnny.

Darby just couldn't forget about Johnny. He had thought that finally he had done something special with a patient and then he just disappeared. He had to know what had happened to Johnny. Everything that he'd believed about their work together and how he'd helped Johnny no longer seemed real. Johnny had just left. Or had he? Darby thought that maybe something was wrong or maybe someone misunderstood something. He had to find out. He just had to. Darby couldn't let himself believe that he had failed again. He had to know for sure.

Darby wished someone would come and explain to him about Johnny. Had he done anything wrong? Darby kept wondering if he had pushed Johnny too hard. He thought and thought about ways he could learn what had happened to Johnny. When he was with his patients, Darby avoided getting attached like he had with Johnny. Johnny just disappearing had affected the way Darby was now working with the patients. He was far more cautious than he used to be.

On day in early spring, as he was exercising in the pasture, Darby decided the 'not knowing' had gone on too long. Darby was determined that today he would find out what happened to Johnny. Why had nobody thought to tell him? Did they think he hadn't noticed that he'd lost his most important patient? If something bad had happened, he wondered if they thought Darby couldn't understand. That made Darby mad and more determined to find out where Johnny was and what had happened. It had been months and Darby didn't know any more than the first day Johnny didn't come to HOPE.

Terry walked around the corner of the barn and Darby decided he'd have to get his attention. *Okay*, thought Darby, *here we go*. He cantered around the center of the pasture and then headed directly for the fence. He might be older, but that fence was only five feet tall and Darby had been sailing over fences that high since he was a colt. *Okay*, he thought, *Terry can see me from where he is right now. He's actually looking at me right now.*

"What is Darby doing?" Terry called to Julie who was now also watching Darby approach the fence. Before she could answer Darby approached the fence, pushed off and sailed over it, missing it by at least a foot.

"Did you see that?" Julie called to Terry. "What's he trying to do?" she yelled as she ran toward Terry. "I've seen him jump before but never that high. I'll go and catch him," she said as she started to run to the pasture area where Darby was standing trying to decide what to do next. Then he began kicking his hind legs and breaking into a full gallop away from Julie. *I want to talk to Terry*, Darby thought. *Julie won't approach me if I start doing crazy things.*

Sure enough, Julie stopped coming toward him. "Terry, I think you need to get him. He's acting a little crazy and he always reacts better with you."

"You're right," said Terry who took off running toward Darby. "Quiet down boy," yelled Terry. "It's okay, Darby, calm down boy. It's okay," Terry said as he began to get near to Darby who was standing and pawing the ground with his front right hoof.

"What is it fellow?" Terry asked as he approached and reached out for Darby's halter. "You obviously want some attention and, I'll tell you, that jump sure got mine." Darby shook his head up and down. "I got it big guy. There's something on your mind, right?" asked Terry as he reached up for Darby's mane only to find the horse shaking his head up and down. "Okay," said Terry. "You've got my attention. Now we have to figure out what you want."

Darby began to walk with Terry beside him, not holding his halter. He'd come to the pasture so fast that he hadn't gotten a lead. Besides, he knew Darby didn't need a lead except when he was working with a patient. Julie stood there with a questioning look on her face. She wondered what was going on between Darby and Terry, but she went back to the barn as the big horse and the boss here at HOPE walked toward the office.

As Darby approached the office building, he went directly to the wheel chair ramp, walking up it to the front door. "Whoa boy," Terry said as he ran up to Darby. "Wait a minute. Why are we here? Darby the last time you led me here it was to find out about Johnny. Is that who you are concerned about?" Terry was talking out loud, but he saw that Darby was nodding a big "Yes".

"Darby," Terry said patting the horse on his neck. "Johnny isn't our patient anymore. You did all you could, but he just left Honor House. Bryan told me that Johnny got a phone call and just left."

"No," Darby moved his head back and forth. As he tried to communicate with Terry, Darby was sure that Johnny wouldn't have just left. He was getting better. Darby knew he was and he wouldn't just leave without a really good reason. Darby put his head on Terry's shoulder, then he nudged his shoulder very hard, almost knocking Terry over.

"What's going on boy?" Terry asked as he pulled back away from Darby, not wanting to be hit again. Darby stepped forward and pushed Terry again. "Quit it Darby," Terry yelled and then he stopped short. "Oh, you're pushing me into the office. "You want me to do something. Is that it Darby?"

While still gently pushing Terry, Darby stopped and shook his head in a clear "Yes" up and down motion.

"I'll tell you what I'll do and you can tell me if that will help. Okay boy?" Terry asked as he turned to go into the office. Darby waited outside as Terry turned and said, "I'll call Bryan, they should be back at Honor House by now. Let's see if he's heard from Johnny. But don't get your hopes up. Most of the times these guys who have been so wounded with PTSD just can't get over their depression and they just leave. We can't save them all, no matter how hard we try." He looked at Darby before he turned to walk to the phone.

Darby stood very still, waiting for Terry to come back. He was so sure that he and Johnny had accomplished a lot. Johnny had finally seemed to understand his depression and how to deal with it better than any patient Darby had ever had before. *Surely, he hadn't just left and gone to live on the streets, homeless*, Darby thought. Some of the really wounded veterans did that. Darby had heard the people at HOPE talking about that. *It was so sad but surely not Johnny*, Darby thought. *Surely not Johnny, without a home!* Just then Terry came out of the office door.

"Well, you were right boy. You were right to make me call," Terry said as he walked to where Darby was still standing. "Johnny did call Bryan, after leaving. He told Bryan that he'd gotten a call that his father was very ill. He had to go immediately as he'd been told his father might not make it. So, he left without talking to anyone," Terry walked up to Darby and the therapy horse put his head gently on Terry's shoulder and leaned his face against Terry's as if to say, "Thank you."

"Darby," Terry said, "the call was a very good sign that Johnny was much better. Even with the concern for his father, he remembered to call Honor House. Johnny said something that seemed very strange to Bryan. He asked Bryan to tell you he had called and what had happened. Bryan said he planned to tell me about Johnny's call when he came out next Wednesday. Everyone at Honor House had been wondering all these months as well, but it seems to be a good sign. Johnny was thinking about others and particularly you, Darby." At that Terry patted Darby's neck, looking directly in his eyes. "You're something else, Darby. I've never been privileged to know a horse like you before."

That night Darby stood in his stall and thought back about his time with Johnny. *That patient became my friend,* thought Darby. *and I did help him. I really did help him.* He stopped at that thought and walked across his stall to take a drink of water. Then, he thought back. *I wonder what I learned from Johnny that I can use with other patients. I wonder if I'll ever have another patient that can understand how I could help him as well as Johnny did.* Then, as he remembered his friend and how good it felt to have at least some success with a patient, he drifted off to sleep for the night.

The early spring nights and early mornings could still be really chilly for North Florida, but Darby kept working, grateful to have something to do. Working always helped him warm up and then his hind quarters wouldn't hurt. He'd begun to have pain more often than before, particularly when it was cold.

Darby continued to work and trying to use some of the communication skills he'd used with Johnny when he was with his adult patients. Sometimes, someone would understand what he was trying to say but usually they just thought he was acting differently from the other horses at HOPE. Darby wished he could bring to his other patients, either children or the veterans, the sense of understanding that he believed Johnny had felt. He'd ask himself, *Was Johnny really as much better as I thought he was or was I just fooling myself.*

Chapter 11

Spring had finally really begun to show off in Florida. The bright sun was shining more often. Everything began to turn green and the red bud trees were starting to be covered with buds. It had been a hard winter for Darby. The cold had kept him uncomfortable with the arthritis in his hind quarters. While he hadn't forgotten Johnny, he'd begun to make peace with the fact that he'd never know what had finally happened to him or if he'd really been able to help him. He was trying to learn to take some pleasure when his patients seemed to enjoy their time with him.

One day, when he was in the pasture he saw little white wild flowers blooming in the woods nearby. They were so delicate but always appeared to show their blossoms among the deep green of the woods. He was just standing in the pasture near the fence that was beside the woods. He loved the smell of spring.

As Darby inhaled a big breath of fresh spring air he heard a car coming down the gravel road which always announced that visitors were approaching. It was a big dark blue car. Darby thought to himself that he'd never seen that car before.

Just then the car turned into the parking area in front of HOPE. *Must be a new patient*, Darby thought, as he intently watched to see who was getting out of the car. *I hope it is a new patient for me. I need some new challenges. I've noticed I'm getting less and less interested in my work and maybe a new challenge would be good for me. Oh well*, he thought, as he moved away from the fence and began to exercise, running to the other side of the pasture where the watering barrel was located.

After a good long drink Darby turned and looked toward the strange car. A man had gotten out and he and Terry were walking toward his pasture. Darby stopped and looked closer at the man. There was something very familiar about him. The man was dressed differently from most of the patients who came to HOPE. He walked with confidence, talking to Terry the entire time. He was coming to the pasture where Darby had been exercising and, in a flash, Darby recognized him. It was Johnny. He was back.

Darby began running across the pasture to where the two men were now standing by the gate. He forgot the pain he'd been experiencing with every step. He forgot everything but Johnny and how he loved this man.

As Darby got to the gate, Johnny had opened it and was standing there, arms wide open, ready to hug his old friend. Darby stopped short right in front of Johnny who reached up and hugged the big horse around his neck. Darby laid his head on Johnny's shoulder, leaning his face against Johnny's cheek. The two stood there for a long time, a reunion that brought tears to Terry's eyes.

"How are you boy," asked Johnny. "I've really missed you and am so sorry I had to leave without telling you. My Dad was very sick, and in fact, he died last month. Darby, with what I had learned from you, I knew I needed to be with him. I'm afraid when I was so sick, I wasn't always kind to him and he had done so much for me," Johnny told Darby. "Darby, I loved my Dad and I wanted him to know that I was getting better. I know he worried about me when I was so messed up. Before he died, I got to tell him all about you and all you had done to help me, you big lug." With his arms still around Darby's neck Johnny looked right into Darby's eyes and said, "I love you my old friend and I missed you." Then Johnny turned back to Terry.

"This horse saved my life, Terry. He taught me how to feel again and to remember how to love and care for others. I owe him my life," Johnny continued as he turned back to Darby. "Boy, I have a lot to tell you."

At that Terry felt he should leave the two old friends alone. He handed Johnny the lead he'd brought to the pasture with him. Johnny thanked him as he pulled a big red apple out of his coat pocket. As he handed the apple to Darby he said, "I remembered that you like these," he said. Darby shook his head up and down as if to say, "You bet I do but most of all I love that you've come back."

"Darby, I have so much to tell you I don't know where to begin," said Johnny. "First, while I still struggle with the PTSD, I've mostly beaten it and begun to move forward with my life. I actually like living again and that is all your doing." Johnny stopped, looking Darby directly in the eyes and running his hand down Darby's neck. "I am better. You taught me how to talk about what I was feeling and you listened. Boy, did you listen, and I knew somehow that you understood. You did understand, didn't you Darby?" Johnny asked.

The horse's head went up and down in a strong affirmative saying, "Yes, I understood." The happiness welled up in Darby and he nuzzled Johnny again. He wished he could say, "Yes, Johnny, I understood what you were going through and I am so happy you're here again with me.

"Darby, I've got lots of news I just have to share with you, my very best friend," Johnny told him with an air of excitement. "I've missed you, my friend. There have been times that I just needed to talk with you. Oh," he said as if there was something that needed to be said, "I forgot to tell you that I talked with Terry a few days ago but I told him not to tell you. I wanted to surprise you. I think I did too." Darby nodded in agreement.

"Well boy, I've got some news to share with you. You know, my Dad was so happy that I was getting better. He loved the stories about how you got me to talk and your crazy antics to make me understand that you knew what I was going through. I'm not sure he believed how we communicated but he did leave a gift for you."

For me, thought Darby. *What could somebody give me, well besides a bushel of apples?*

"Darby listen to me," said Johnny as he brought Darby's face close to his and looked directly in his eyes. "Darby, my Dad had a wonderful farm with a barn that is heated and big enough to be an indoor riding ring. Before he died he called his lawyer to come into his hospital room. I know you probably don't know what a lawyer is but he's a guy who helps people communicate their wishes for what happens to what they have, after they have died. That's called a will." Johnny looked at Darby to make sure he understood.

Darby was still watching and listening. He knew what 'died' meant. It was when someone went away and would never return. That's how Darby understood the word. He'd never thought about what happened to their stuff. *That wasn't much of a problem for a horse*, Darby thought. When his friend died at the hunter stable, they gave Darby his halter, but it was a little too small. Darby assumed that one of the smaller horses got it.

Darby was lost in thought about his friend at the hunter stable when suddenly he realized that Johnny was still talking. "Darby," said Johnny as he had noticed that he'd lost Darby's attention. "Darby, Dad had the lawyer change his will before he died. It is a beautiful farm and you my friend are going to live there with me."

Darby wasn't sure he understood what Johnny had said. Johnny could see that Darby wasn't quite understanding, after all, this was a huge thing. "Darby," said Johnny, holding the big horse's face in his hands. "Darby, you are coming to live with me on the farm my Dad gave me."

Hardly believing what he was hearing, Darby thought, *but I live at HOPE. I work at HOPE,* he thought. *Can I just go with Johnny and live at this farm he has? How is this possible*, he wondered?

"Darby, I just bought you from HOPE," Johnny held his face again as he spoke. "I know that you have arthritis and are often in pain, particularly in the cold. It is time for you to be able to retire. Oh, don't worry, there will be people you can help from your new home but I will see to it that your hind quarters don't hurt anymore, just like you helped me not to hurt so much."

Darby shook his head side to side as if to say, *I don't understand. Are you telling me that you've come back, not to work with me but to take me home with you? This will take some getting used to*, thought Darby.

"Darby, you saved my life," Johnny said. "The least I can do is make yours more comfortable and I do want you with me during your retirement. You've worked hard your entire life, my friend, now it's time for you to enjoy life a little." Johnny stopped and hugged the big horse around the neck. "It is because of you that I can live again. I love you big guy," Johnny said as he released the hug and began rubbing Darby's neck. "Don't worry Darby, HOPE will be able to buy and train at least two new therapy horses with what I gave them for you." Then Johnny stopped and thought about how much this all was for Darby to understand in just this short time. Looking Darby in the eyes again, just like Darby had always insisted when he was a patient, Johnny said, "Of course, there will never be another therapy horse like Darby but I know they will try."

Johnny hooked the lead to Darby's halter and the two began to walk back to the stable. "Darby, I will be back tomorrow with a trailer for you to ride back to my farm. I've made arrangements with stables along the way so we can stop and let you exercise and rest every so many hours as we make our way to your new home." Johnny explained all of his plans as they walked back to the stable.

"Darby, you taught me so many things. First, I learned that I still had to find a place to be of service to other people. I've enrolled in a graduate program. Oh, that might not mean anything to you," Johnny said and then stopped to think how to put it. "I'm going back to school to learn how to become a hospital administrator," Johnny explained. "While I still don't want to practice medicine, I want to learn to make sure that hospital's where people go when they are very sick, can do the best job possible to provide good care for their patients. What do you think, boy?" Johnny asked.

While Darby didn't understand all that Johnny had said but he'd heard the words good care and patients and he kind of understood. He felt like it was really good that Johnny was preparing for a future and one of helping others, just like a therapy horse. Darby also understood going to school as he had done when he first began to be a Therapy horse. He had to learn how to help people and he did. *Johnny would too*, Darby thought.

Terry was waiting for them back beside Darby's stall. "Well, Darby," Terry spoke softly in Darby's ear. "I guess you know about your new life with Johnny."

Darby shook his head up and down in a resounding "Yes". Inside, Darby wasn't sure how he felt about leaving HOPE but he did know he was so happy to see Johnny, happier than he'd been for a very long time. As he thought about his life and how it would be to be retired and in a heated barn. Darby thought, *This might be a wonderful life.* Then he remembered how he'd questioned if he'd ever been successful. Now all he had to do was look at Johnny to know his life had mattered. Darby had become a success and was being rewarded by the man he loved most.

"Darby," said Johnny, "I forgot to tell you. We have a new addition at the farm. Last week, I saw him for the first time as he flew right overhead. The next day I saw him again as he flew into one of the big trees beside the fields that are behind the barn. Darby, we have a huge bald eagle that has just made his home next to the barn at the farm where you and I will live. He was so majestic and seemed to be looking for something at the farm. He'll be there when we get to your new home. It's like he's waiting for you."

The big gray horse lifted his head to look Johnny right in the eye. For once, he really wished he could talk. You see, Darby remembered the eagle and now he knew what the eagle had been trying to tell him. The eagle wanted him to know that he was going to have a very special patient, one who had served his country well and now needed Darby's help. Darby was pleased that his eagle friend had made his home near Johnny's farm. Now he knew that his life had mattered and the giant eagle was waiting to tell him so. They'd live at Johnny's farm, the hero, his therapy horse, and the bird that symbolized why they were there, all together.